NOTES FROM "*The Catacombs*"

NOTES FROM "The Catacombs"

A CRITIQUE OF THE CHRISTIAN CHURCH

T HANS

Primix Publishing
East Brunswick Office Evolution
1 Tower Center Boulevard, Ste 1510
East Brunswick, NJ 08816
www.primixpublishing.com
Phone: 1-800-538-5788

© 2025 T Hans. All rights reserved.

No part of this book may be reproduced, stored in a retrieval system, or transmitted by any means without the written permission of the author.

Published by Primix Publishing: 08/04/2025

ISBN: 979-8-89194-535-7(sc)
ISBN: 979-8-89194-536-4(e)

Library of Congress Control Number: 2025915097

Any people depicted in stock imagery provided by iStock are models, and such images are being used for illustrative purposes only.

Certain stock imagery © iStock.

Because of the dynamic nature of the Internet, any web addresses or links contained in this book may have changed since publication and may no longer be valid. The views expressed in this work are solely those of the author and do not necessarily reflect the views of the publisher, and the publisher hereby disclaims any responsibility for them.

Contents

Introduction vii

An Email To My Representative 1
A Letter To The Editor -- Toward the end of 2006 . . 5
An Email To Dawn 9
A Email To My Son -- 4/27/11 19
Another Letter To My Son -- 5/10/12 23
A Radical Reformation – Moving From
               Words Into Action! 26
Prison Visits... July, 2014 44
An Email To A Lutheran Minister 47
A Second Email To A Lutheran Minister 53
An Email To A Cousin 55
An Email To A Hunger Activist 57
"A Position Paper" -- July 28, 2015 61

Conclusion 89

Introduction

This short but shocking book is spliced together with about a dozen of my personal writings... spread out over a number of years. All of these written statements were "stirred up" or "rose from the dead" because of an honest concern for finding Christian truth in troublesome times. They all spring from a straightforward study of the New Testament... and how that ancient testimony relates so beautifully to concrete living in contemporary society. Nothing in this book is "written in stone", since our human perspective is continually changing and learning new truths as time moves on. However, that is not to say that what I have written is not relevant or appropriate for living in the here and now. It is truth for today. These presented comments could be accepted and implemented now for a more profound, rewarding and divine existence, and/or absorbed and promoted in the future for a "heavenly existence" on this wonderful planet.

The title, Notes From "The Catacombs" comes from a sincere conviction that the Christian Church (or maybe even more broadly -- the contemporary Christian faith) has "missed the boat" as to the intentions of Jesus Christ. The Jesus of the New Testament (who spoke so eloquently and lived so divinely) --this Jesus wanted his followers to follow his lead in their activities -- their daily living. He did not want them to worship him for his forgiveness and generous, gracious gifts. Where present day church goers enjoy their buildings and comfortable pews, hear words encouraging present, convenient lifestyles, are taught to trust in the world's perspectives, identify their spiritual values and ideals with the structured church's traditions, and finally, (and maybe most sadly) are driven to keep up "playing church" by the promise of eternal life after death -- Jesus had no intention that this would be his legacy. It's all really very simple... according to the Bible. Jesus came to earth as a self-giving servant to show people how to live in love. His Father had created the world so that his creation could live in peace, love and happiness -- a "garden of Eden" existence. However, human beings wanted to run the show, so they ran into problems. When God's Son, Jesus, arrived, he tried to teach people how to get along with one another. Here was a concrete earthly example from God himself. But when they again insisted on doing things their own way and looking to him for what they thought was important, He made clear He had not come for that purpose. The crowds (his "church") crucified him, since there would not be free meals and a grand promise of eternal bliss. No wonder Jesus was so distraught! They never got the point of divine living --self-giving, love, forgiveness and servant-hood. Yes, Jesus' example of life and living got buried with him in the Catacombs and His Spirit is still there today. After He died, conveniently, the Christian

Church "resurrected Jesus" to have him give their loyal members all they ever wanted -- a blessed life, material security, a social club, forgiveness, sacraments, worship centers, A Holy One to worship, and above all, eternal life. They would sing his praises until he would come again and carry them home. "Take your ease, eat, drink and be merry!" It has been said before... with the warning about death without hope. Yes, the Christian Church has "missed the boat".

Now this bad news is not easy to take. We want good news -- we like that the historical Church has made the New Testament a voice of comfortable convenience. Who doesn't love grace... plus, eternal life!? Through the ages, the Church has had its benefits from this, of course. But consider the real loss to the world... with no answers but man's selfish ones, say nothing of the distressing copycat religions who have also taken their "cuts" and secured outrageous offerings with the promise of a better life beyond. It's all very sad! Will our distressed planet ever recover from throwing away this "buried treasure"? Will the world's real treasure ever be uncovered and brought to light? Will we ever have our small planet redeemed and restored?

Why should I write this book? Who cares? Who wants to hear the unvarnished truth... as I (little man that I am) see it? These things are too radical, too preposterous and too unsettling for anyone today. Even deep within I have mixed feelings. How can I be right, no matter how convinced I might be that I know that the love of Jesus Christ really does work... and that it is indeed the hope of the world. Why shouldn't we all just flow along for centuries on the tide of man's instincts? Let's all just do what feels good and what other people applaud. Right? But then I remember the story Jesus told about "sowing the seed." The planter goes out to sow the seed, knowing that all the seed will not land in fertile soil. In fact, very little will take root and be fruitful. I must acknowledge that I am called to sow some seed, even though I may be doubtful about the results. So I also must ask myself, what will be the loss if I lay out this book for whatever or whoever? I will do as I am guided in my ministry, whatever the risks.

I must admit that I am not afraid of what people might think or of unknown consequences. Today, I strive to find the truth as best I can know that truth in my time and place. I must affirm that the death of Jesus has not been nor is it debatable. The dictionary tells us that The Catacombs were underground cemeteries near Rome. Some of these cemeteries were used as a refuge for early Christians. So we know that people died and were buried. Jesus was crucified, died and was buried. What, if anything, was raised? For what purpose? The resurrection is what's up for discussion.

The following presentations and emails are all related to my life and living. They also speak in special ways to the activities that call for my attention. They are not all life and death issues, but they all do relate to the inspiration I receive from the central story of Jesus' life on this planet, so many years ago. History speaks to me and I must respond as best I can, even as Jesus related to the people and situations he ran into on his daily travels. I cannot and will not avoid or overlook my connection to my Lord and leader. His Spirit commands my attention. He offers insight. He truly is "the light of the world".

T. Hans Olson 9/15/2015

An Email To My Representative

November 20, 2006
Dear Representative:

We are hearing a lot of argument, discussion and debate about what can be done about the war in Iraq and the so called "war on terrorism." According to present reports by the news media, there are few, if any, satisfactory solutions... especially considering the complexities of the Middle East.

For years we have been trying to gain control of the situation in Iraq with "the stick." Our approach has not been working. In fact, as U.S. citizens, we have lost a lot in human lives, financial resources and international good will... say nothing about what the people of Iraq have experienced and witnessed. I would like to propose a solution to this difficult situation using "the carrot". The solution is simple and is almost certain to work satisfactorily. It only requires a certain degree of insight by our leaders in Washington.

I would propose we withdraw our military forces from Iraq immediately (or as soon as possible). Our government would suggest to the government and people of Iraq that as soon as the U.S. military is out of the country, we freely offer to send in a "restoration team" to work toward the complete rehabilitation of the Iraqi oil fields -- for one year and one year only. The purpose would be to get the country back on its feet financially... with every man woman and child sharing in the oil profits. We would be willing to use a good portion of the money we are presently putting into the war... to provide needed repairs and development toward the goal that all the people of Iraq rest on a solid financial footing. We would indicate that we have no desire for political influence or economic gain. If our workers were not able to do their work safely and efficiently, this "restoration team" would simply leave and let the people of Iraq deal with their own problems. End of story.

This proposal would certainly accomplish a number of important objectives that would be beneficial to the U.S. as well as to the people of Iraq.

A few of the benefits for the American people: 1. It would get us out of a troublesome war (and loss of American lives) immediately. 2. It would stop our part in the killing and save us billions of dollars attempting to force our will on another people and culture. 3. It would begin to fight "the war on terrorism" in a new way... with goodwill. 4. It would indicate our desire to help all the people of Iraq... as well as to start to rehabilitate their country. 5. It would give us "a time certain" to cut our expenses in Iraq. 6. It would help us rebuild our international standing and give new insight into the wisdom and friendliness of the American people. 7. It would be a new, non-partisan method of accomplishing all our goals. 8. It probably would help more quickly bring to the market some presently unavailable oil reserves. 9. It might give us a bit of good will to help deal with some of the other difficult problems in the Middle East.

Some of the benefits for the people of Iraq: 1. It would end foreign intervention and domination immediately. 2. It would put the responsibility of government, law, politics, sectarianism and future development in their own hands... for better or for worse. 3. It would give them a financial incentive to stop the violence and keep "the American rehabilitation team" safe and happy. They would strongly desire our presence rather than question our commitments and motives. 4. It would help the divided people of that land see that goodness and kindness can come out of a democracy... where people compromise and work together. 5. It would give a positive incentive (to all the people of that war torn land) to work together to rebuild their society... since all would benefit. 6. It would give the people of Iraq "a whole new ballgame" to consider... and give them a glimpse of hope for the future.

The benefits for our two societies and for the world are clear... especially since carrying on our past methods will almost certainly lead to very negative consequences, maybe indefinitely. The time is ripe for a change in our approach to bringing peace, happiness and security to all people. We should not proceed with "a fortress mentality", if for no other reason than that we will eventually lose! The U.S. could use "a new image" on this small planet where people are so interdependent. In our age of "global warming", we as human beings will either learn to understand one another, work together and live in peace... or we will die in contention and insecurity with a very short future. It's time for a new image -- of a wise, caring, responsible, sharing people. It's time to look honestly, carefully and extensively at a cost/benefit sheet. Truly great leaders will take the initiative to speak up with fresh insight into what can work successfully in this new age of the 21st century. We look at Martin Luther King as one example from the past.

For the sake of the American people and even for the sake of the whole world, please consider some fresh approaches to the problems we face in our international relationships. History takes note of favorable turning points and dynamic leadership. Certainly "a carrot" is needed and could be "tasty" for these troublesome times.

Sincerely... with hope,

T. Hans Olson
The Change Agent
Eau Claire, WI 54703

A Letter To The Editor --
Toward the end of 2006

Letters To The Editor are popular reading material in our small city newspaper. I live in an upper Midwest area of the United States. Our beautiful city is a fairly conservative community where there are probably as many churches as there are bars. People are friendly, we have good public schools and an excellent university, the crime rate is low, music and the arts flourish, there is a very reasonable cost of living and our city has been considered one of the best places to raise a family. We have it good here, and people take pride in being responsible citizens, caring neighbors and fair minded human beings. What's not to like? One might think there would be very little controversy in the editorial section of the local paper, but that would be wrong. As in today's world, there is an independent way of thinking that's very prevalent, and consequently, there are many viewpoints expressed in the letters presented daily. Over the years, I too have had a couple of letters published.

Back a few years, it occurred to me that our "Christian fundamentals" are often very much at odds with our proclamations and practices in daily living. Church people testify that Jesus has the answers for life and living, that we should be his followers and that we will "get to heaven" through faith or trusting in Him. We believe that Bible study is important for learning about Jesus and what he expects of his followers. But what does a community like ours really think and stand for? In a nice little city such as ours, is it worthwhile to ask questions that seek to examine our credibility and our practices? Is that a bad thing to do? Most of us who claim to be Christian argue that we would be willing to "fight to the death" rather than give up a fundamental Christian principle. Would we do this, or do our political activities (the practical life of the city/state) trump our spiritual convictions? Putting it even more simply, does our daily practical living win out over our spiritual considerations? (It's the world's ways versus God's ways.) Do questions like these reveal a nice "middle of the road" community such as ours as attractive and exemplary? Or, are we the kind of people who don't really want to look at the truth about ourselves? Are we the kind of people who "walk by on the other side"... with reference to the broader scope of things?

Toward the close of the Iraq war, I decided that I would like to contribute a letter to the editor that might stimulate some thinking about our feelings concerning our U.S. military efforts and our moral or spiritual principles. I wanted to be direct, short and clear as well as raise an issue relevant to a good share of the paper's editorial readers. Here's the letter to the editor I sent in -- yes, one simple question. I made sure I signed my name, so there would be no question as to the source.

"Who should love Saddam Hussein?"

I knew that this question could cause some consternation or trouble. But in the beginning, I was not prepared for what happened. The letter was not published. I will not try to imagine what determined the Editor's decision. I can say that potential "problems" were avoided and that the readers of our newspaper were not faced with a difficult question. What a relief for an editor who might have been under some criticism for publishing the question.

Now here's the dilemma. I would guess that almost all the citizens of the U.S. (this grand "Christian nation") had a deep loathing or hatred for Saddam Hussein. After all, he was responsible for carrying out a lot of evil deeds. That need not be debated. He was the poster boy for someone almost every American hated with a vengeance! He exemplified the enemy. Find him! Kill him! The worst punishment would be none too good for Saddam. That was the prevailing sentiment. On the other hand, Jesus tells his followers to "love your enemies"... etc. Jesus did not qualify his declaration -- saying there are limits, qualifications or exceptions. None. Just "love your enemies". From His point of view, there were and are a lot of reasons for his followers to do this (it's the Divine way), but no one needs to wonder about this. Just do it. Period. So the answer to the question is -- all Christians should love Saddam Hussein. (If you want to check out the reasoning, do some research in the New Testament.) Finally, the question for the so called "Christian community" is, who are we really following? Whose "marching orders" do we implement?

What guides our thinking about people... and war... and retribution, etc.? Is it "the world's viewpoint" or is it "the Divine viewpoint"? Are we headed for hell... or for heaven? Now that's the dilemma!

An Email To Dawn

(A High School classmate)
On Tuesday, June 8, 2010 at 1:04 AM, Hans Olson wrote:

Dawn...

What a nice surprise! I didn't realize my Class Reunion "highlights" would go out by email, but it's a real plus to hear from someone like you.

You said you "have a couple of questions." Frankly, even I'd have a lot of questions about what I wrote... not that I would necessarily qualify or change anything at the moment, but life is pretty complicated and confusing at times. And then one looks at a religion like our Christian religion... and wow! On the other hand, I believe the Christian faith is really quite simple, when it comes right down to it. Jesus Christ... love (agape -- love for the worthless) in the flesh... endless forgiveness... hope for the future... relying on/trusting the creator of it all... being thankful for all we have been given... redemption/freedom/salvation as human beings -- things such as these are really quite understandable and simple... and at the heart of our Christian faith. What's not so easy is to be a "little Christ" or one of His followers. And that's because we get all wrapped up in ourselves (even like the apostles) -- we are self-centered or sinful human beings. We get to thinking "it's all about me" and my own happiness... and my own point of view... and my own connections... and even my own personal future/ heaven. How different is that than the motivation the terrorists have of giving up their lives in order to go to "heaven" and enjoy all the benefits!? Pretty self-centered and utterly dependent on a personal, vindictive god. I think we are to be motivated to want to live-- as well as to love and be creative --to bring new life and Jesus to the world. Too bad that the terrorists don't have a chance to come to know the goodness and grace of Jesus. How sad. Mostly, we "Christians" just give them more of the law, judgment and threats they already know and carry out. Who should love Saddam Hussein? Where would you have heard that awhile back? Nowhere! Not even in Eau Claire. But that's basic: Love your enemies. Of course, following Jesus means continually trying to walk in his footsteps and take his side as we confront the world around us. That's 180 degrees different than what the world shows us. It's not so complicated, but it is revolutionary! What would life be like if we weren't so into ourselves and cheering for "the survival of the fittest"/the jungle mentality!? I believe Jesus Christ was God's Word to us... about a different way of life that would highlight the Creator God's intention from the beginning. But then, today, we have before us the Pope, cathedrals, abusers, military might, egocentric personal testimonies, games of murder, "God's on our side" nationalistic propaganda, drugs to escape, charities to pad pocketbooks, personal retribution, etc. -- all supported by people calling themselves "Christians". That's the cross Jesus is crucified on... in our day and age! It's almost enough to make me want to "throw up" or run away. Now, that's just my general perspective from reading the Bible.

You are right. We are told to plant the seed and be faithful and wait for the harvest in God's own time. I will never fully understand just how God works. Nevertheless, we also know that The Holy Spirit is at work in this world among Christ's followers and that His work is evident if we want to look for it. The Holy Spirit is not off in the clouds somewhere, and if He can't be seen at work in this world, then we can be certain that God is dead! I can only testify... that generally, church goers do not speak up for Jesus and say...."the Holy Spirit was among us today, and I have been altered/changed/inspired for Jesus sake and for the Kingdom of God." Where is the Holy Spirit among us... as we keep our mouths closed about the radical Word... and do not speak of thankfulness... and as we give our self-serving crumbs like the rich man... and do not stop for the man beaten by the side of the road... and as we put our personal politics ahead of Christ-like priorities? Yes, we will wait for the ultimate judgment; but in the present, we are never meant to yield to the world's destructive behavior. We are called to highlight Jesus' behavior, not deny his Divine perspectives and actions. Jesus Christ and His Holy Spirit were presented to us as a gift to bring new life to those dying and sitting in darkness. He's not a cheerleader for the rich and powerful and famous! Such people don't want a savior or someone to lead them, because they take care of themselves. I believe God is alive and well today; but be certain, at least if we want to go by the Bible, He is active in the most surprising times and places. How many people listened to Amos in his day (almost a carbon copy of our own time and place) or how many people rallied around Jesus on the cross? Don't trust in the majority vote, if you want to be on the side of Jesus.

The Christian Church today is of our own making -- from our glamorous church buildings... to our materially secure pastoral leadership... to our comfortable pews... to our sentimental, professionalized songs... to our hour long Sunday Schools... to our capitalistic Christmas celebrations... to our dying chain of spiritual authority... to our watering down of The Scriptures... to good time, entertainment Sunday services... to well, you get the picture! It's of our own making -- it's does not come out of "the Jesus tradition". What connection do the above have to do with a new way of looking and life and a new way of living? How do the above lead us to living on less and sacrifice for others and caring for God's planet? It's really a popularized, selfish religion that takes us down the wrong road. It's not The Word made flesh (God's Word made flesh). A new reformation would reverse the self-destruction of the world, rely on acting out God's Word and move away from a focus on words, words, words! The old Reformation did get us to the point of intellectually understanding what the Bible was about. The problem today is not about who Jesus is and about his message. The problem is about implementing or acting out God's Word. Jesus--the real Jesus-- is essentially not to be found "in the flesh" today --certainly not generally in the structured church. The church is just too popular and too rewarding. What did the people want on Palm Sunday? A King who would give them all they wanted --certainly security and power and eternal happiness! The whole point of Jesus coming in the flesh was to act out His Word and show us how to live and love...radically, redemptively and creatively... here and now... for the sake of God's world! Who will lead us -- the politicians, the entertainers, the professors, the teachers, the lawyers, the doctors, the scientists, the historians, the bishops... or even the ministers? Who can we trust to step out and lead us to ACT for the sake of Jesus Christ and for new life in the world? Who will show us a different way than the way the world points? Who has led, who leads and who will lead... inspired by God... in the work of the Holy Spirit?

You can be sure I wouldn't be saying any of this if I thought "God is dead". But certainly God is struggling "for a place to stay" in many individual hearts and souls. The churched masses, like the tides, just seem to push or pull people down into the least common denominator. Certainly, a lot of "God's people" are once again heading off down a dead end street... and feeling pretty self-righteous about themselves and where they are headed... with the blessings of the clergy. The clergy too want their earthly security. I do not doubt your "credentials" for being a good Christian or a good person. I don't doubt that you know where God wants you to be. It's great that you are thankful and feel very blessed. I too feel thankful and richly blessed. Yet, it's also important that I understand how the world (the average person) might look at me... yes, as disgusting, etc. or... as the classmate that "didn't turn out so good". I want to acknowledge that... and in fact, I take some pride in being "a rebel" or someone some people think "has gone off the deep end". You can't help but be offended by at least some of what I'm saying. I'm even offended by my own comments. I am not a saint. I'm only called to be a servant of our Lord. Truly, Jesus is the Way, the Truth and the Life! And if I want to claim to be a Christ-follower, I need to speak the Truth and then try to act on it! I am called out to do so. Being a little presumptuous, I have a thought that you too sometimes might feel a little bit "a rebel". Take some pride in that. In our time and place, Christ-followers (little Christs, servants, lovers) are rebels! Look at our world! There's no way around it.

I really like and applaud your last six line paragraph! You have a lot to offer your family, your friends, your classmates and the whole world around you. I would guess that you are a person growing each day in your understanding of who you are, where you are headed and how you can help others. Cheers!

I hope I haven't disturbed you too much. I know that usually the best kind of questioning/opening up/change/adjustment in thinking, etc. takes place slowly (St. Paul being an obvious exception) for all of us.

My book "A Bible Story" is not available in bookstores because I wanted it to be based on actual translations of the Bible and not on my subjective interpretations. I did translate a number of passages where I felt I could clarify the original texts, but for the most part the verses are what most Bible lovers remember and treasure. What I have done is take out all duplications and tell the story of the New Testament without "books" and with supporting evidence from the Old Testament. Many Psalms have their place as well as the Prophets. In short, no publishing house would permit me to use their translations, except for a few copies. What I will do for you is attempt to let you visualize "A Bible Story".

The cover is soft and colorful... in white -- upper right hand corner -- "A Bible Story". Slightly below that on the top left -- Jesus Is Lord! The background shows a distant high mountain covered with snow. It fades, drifting down to lower levels; and closer to the bottom you see the tips of green trees. A rainbow goes from the top left corner down to the bottom right corner...through "Jesus Is Lord!"... and down through the following words top to bottom... Loving Believing Growing Praising Thanking Changing Following Confessing Sacrificing Witnessing Receiving Promising Forgiving Suffering Blessing Striving Healing Trusting Waiting Serving Praising Obeying Giving Sowing Rising Calling Hoping. The colorful, hopeful rainbow flows through them all.

There are six translations in this book -- all noted by initials...including my own. Features: 26 in all...It all starts with Jesus... and ends with love. Love and gospel overpower selfishness and law. It summarizes Biblical truth in Bible words. Five different versions of the Bible are quoted. A general time-line is laid out to aid understanding. Repetition and less important passages are left out. Narrow historical perspectives are omitted. It focuses on New Testament essentials for the 20th century. A Christian perspective--central religious and spiritual truth. It blends many "letters" together for today's Christians. Similar passages are organized together to complement one another. "Treasured passages" are finally identified and bracketed. Passages are interpreted generally by placement in chapters. It offers interesting transitional reading one passage after another. It encourages Bible reading--compact, interesting, delightful, surprising. A resource for Bible study with special translations. It pulls passages out of context to focus attention on "the center". An emphasis is on the positive in passage selection. Favorite passages are easy to find and understand. Motivation and inspiration--heavy "carrot" and light "stick. The Bible through "a prophet's" eyes. A great witness for the kind of change Jesus came to reveal. A resource for "new life and living." The organizer's "top ten" Bible passages--or pick your own. Easy to put down and pick up for small time slots. A good gift idea for meditation, inspiration, study and discussion.

Next comes the Prologue. From the internet --"A Baby's Hug". "A Bible Story" is meant to reveal the Spirit of love... as well as reach deep into our hearts and minds to foster discipleship.

Christian Highlights: The Bible For The 20th Century... Good News For Life And Living... Your

Favorite Passages... Inspirational Insights!... The Best Of The Best... The Way To Love... The Gift Of Love.

Chapters: Section 1--Jesus arrives... Jesus is God's Son... Jesus speaks with authority... Jesus' death and resurrection... Section 2--The Holy Spirit... Saul is changed to Paul... The Church--The Body of Christ... Section 3--The Law... Judgment... Justice... The Good News--The Gospel... Choice... Section 4--Humility... Commitment... Mission... Section 5--Lifestyle... Worship... Baptism/Confession... Grace/Forgiveness... Change... Comfort. Section 6--New Life and Healing... Thankfulness... Faith... Hope... Love

There are 215 pages. References come next: Passages and page numbers are evident for every Old and New Testament book that is included.

I have selected what I consider to be the "Top Ten" passages in the Bible. I also note the next 20 great passages in the Old and New Testaments. And finally, I also highlight the final 20 most loved passages. There are 50 in all. Of course, I encourage each person to pick out their own favorite portions of Scripture.

On page 227, I list "Special Words" and the number of occurrences in "A Bible Story". Those alphabetized words go from "Action" to "Worship". God occurs 755 times, Jesus 459 times... down to Patience 11 times and Confess 13 times.

I end with Sunday -- March 12, 2006, 9:00 am. Last night I had "a dream," which had a significant impact on me......

Page 230 ends: 3/30/06 Being a Christian isn't just "changing", as good as that might be! Following Jesus is being in the process of doing a lot of divine "little things"--following in the footsteps of our Lord. My cover will reflect that truth.

Well Dawn, that's it! I'm not sure I answered all the questions you asked. I probably gave you much more than you wanted. Are you still with me? :-) But thank you for your interest and concern. You spoke up. Do as you wish with the above. As you said, "....I think we are way past putting on airs about who we are."

A classmate and friend, Hans

A Email To My Son -- 4/27/11

Dear Awesome Son, Luther...

Thanks for your comments about Facebook and the "thank you". Since I probably won't come down tomorrow and have a chance to talk to you, I figured I should share a few things with you about baptism. Lindsey has talked with us about her feelings about it... and I thought I should pass on to the two of you some of my beliefs and feelings. This "dedication" and/or baptism coming up is certainly a significant event in your life, as well as in Amelia's life. Marian and I are certainly looking forward to it.

Baptism has been and is central to the Christian Church, since the early days. As Lutherans we have focused on "The Word and Sacraments", and rightfully so. The Christian Church throughout the ages has not done much right, but I believe that "that focus" has been good and valid. I was honored to baptize you, Luther, and welcome you into the Christian family and our congregation. Like your birth into our family, you were received with love and status without any merit on your part. That signified unconditional love and grace! I was so happy to hear that your middle name for Amelia was Grace! The most important sacrament for me is baptism because it focuses on God's grace (his agape/love) for us. Certainly He loves us at least as well as we love our children and there's no way we can get away from Him or lose His Love. Jesus has done it all for us, and so all we can do is to say and live "thank you". That's essentially the center of our Christian faith. We simply grow in our understanding of what it means to be a child of God or a Christ follower. We live out "a daily baptism" of being cleansed of our sin (self-centeredness) and coming forth as a "new creature" --washed clean by water and The Spirit and the blood of Jesus given for us. Grace is the center of it all --nothing we learn or testify to or sacrifice for or do, etc. can save us. Martin Luther's life was about finding Grace, where the whole Roman Catholic tradition focused on working or paying or praying your way in. No wonder he was so torn and why his insights into scripture were so valuable. Grace is where it's at and hopefully we come to understand how good it all is. That will be your role as Dad... and Lindsey's role as Mom --to share with Amelia what a wonderful gift she has been given and how vital it is and will be for her life of happiness and fulfillment. You are getting Amelia off "on the right foot", so to speak.

God's grace is on Amelia even now. Baptism is significant for us because it is a tangible expression of an invisible miracle. Sacraments (concrete expressions) are helpful to us in our daily, earthly, mundane activities. God helps us with these earthly activities or events as we venture through life day by day. But they are not "slight of hand" activities (like paying enough to get a soul halfway to heaven) that many people would like. God provides growth (as His creation shows us every year) through dying and rising, confession and forgiveness, finding out our badness and changing. It's all a process of trying to become more like Jesus every day. Now whether you "Dedicate" Amelia and/or Baptize her --that is for you to decide, and you will help her understand what living in the family of our Triune God really means in all its concreteness. Not much is chiseled in stone. Luther, I'm happy you are seeking out what feels right and good for you. Different churches have different traditions and hopefully you tune in with the congregation where you have or will have membership. As of now, I can't offer you a Christian family as a pastor, I can't offer you a baptismal service as a part of a church's tradition, I have no baptismal certificate that's valid in a particular denomination, I can't baptize with the intent that Amelia is becoming a member of "our congregation" nor can I work around another pastor's official duties. I wish I could act as Amelia's pastor, but I cannot. I think you know how much I love and adore Amelia and would like to have a very important place in her life. But I will be very happy with whatever commonplace activities I can rightfully and honestly provide to her and the two of you. I am so happy that both of you are together in your Christian faith and have a common vision of how you want to live out that faith. The important point is not "what kind of celebrations" you go through as a family, but that you do "celebrate", in any way you choose -- the miracle of God's Grace! Move forward in confidence with Peace! Almighty God, the Father, Son and Holy Spirit is with you and sustains you!

Love, Hans, Dad, Grampa

Another Letter To My Son -- 5/10/12

Luther...

I just got off the exercise bike and wanted to convey to you some of my thoughts. I decided it "couldn't wait". Having felt I was called into the Christian ministry, I still feel there are certain truths that our God wants spoken, and this, I feel, comes pretty directly from his Revelation to us. Of course, I too feel there is a little too much "ego" in what I just said, so please take this with "a grain of salt", if that's your inclination. Hopefully this won't be too long! :-)

    You mentioned yesterday, something to the effect that nobody wants to "change"... but also that "change" is a hot topic these days. You are certainly correct on both accounts. The fact that "nobody wants to change" is in good measure the reason we are in such deep trouble these days. Who wants to listen? Who wants to do something different? Who wants to give in to the opposition? Who isn't willing to "fight for their rights"? Look at the political scene... or international conflicts... or religious positions... or even family squabbles? It goes on and on. Almost everyone is "down on the future" and that there is no real long term hope. It's in our biology to "fight for survival" or fight for my interests... and that pretty much is self-centeredness and rebellion against God --going all the way back to Adam and Eve. It's my feeling that the whole Bible is about change... if you want to study it deeply. In fact, the best of God's revelation to us is that Jesus came so that we might be loved and open to change.. so that we too can be flexible in love... and open ourselves to "self-giving"... and seeing the "neighbor" in a different way... and give up a part of ourselves (maybe even unto death as Jesus did) for the sake of "the other side". That's pretty radical and hard to take for most people. After all, we know and believe that as the seed dies unto itself, it rises to new life and produces almost unlimited fruit. I think that all this speaks for self-giving, hopeful, divine flexibility (or willingness to change) rather than self-centered, angry, threatening rigidity (which leads to deterioration, a hellish life and death or extinction). Could it be that for this "new age" and hope for our planet and happiness for all people... that the new Word from the Bible and from Jesus is that "God is change"!? Imagine life on our planet where "change is a friend" --that people could cast off rigidity for flexibility and LEARN to look to the welfare of others... if for no other reason than for survival!? That leads me into this --maybe an even more "scientific truth":

Since the very beginning of time, the whole earth has been in "flux". It was made to change and to be continually changing. The only thing that doesn't seem to change is change itself. God is change. In the end, only the flexible will survive. There are endless examples of where "rigid life forms" did not make it (and they won't today). They went extinct --never to be influential again (except maybe in their death and deterioration... and fuel for the fire). Is this where we are headed today as a human race... to rigid fighting, self-centeredness, contention and inability to see "the bigger picture"?! All of nature and the history of the world teaches us that if we want to live in love, happiness, fulfillment, caretaking and in Divine acceptance, we need to be open to creative change and the continuing flexibility to become what Almighty God wants us to be. We need to be consciously always changing --learning new ways to live in love (in the pattern of Jesus). Only in that way will we "survive" as individuals and as the human race. So, from the Bible, from Jesus, from the history of the world, from nature, from looking honestly and realistically at life on this planet today, from biology, from our experience, we need to look at change as a friend (rather than as the enemy) and try to be flexible in our life and reasoning... so that we might endure and be a blessing to all God has given to us. Obviously, this is easier said than done. This message may never really get out... to get any traction. And we may all go to hell... if not live in it. But in the end, I do know that seeds can die, take root and produce wonderful fruit. In the end, I do have a friend in change (whether I like it or not)... and I do have hope. In a real way, your comments inspired these thoughts. Thanks. Love, Dad

A Radical Reformation – Moving From Words Into Action!

10/15/2012

God Is Love ….Never forcing, always welcoming, attracting

THE TOP TEN (Concepts for Contemplation) –

1. Action-- Action is central to love – it is central to living the Christian life and carrying out Christian priorities. Loving action is central to being a "little Christ". Action is being involved in showing God Is Love. It is implementing the following:

2. Agape-- Father/Creator... Loving... even what is "worthless". Jesus gives us some sense of this when he says "love your enemies". What really is "agape"? Here's a vivid example: I lived on a farm in central Wisconsin where we raised pigs. Pigs ate and slept in our big barn -- out of sight. They

had automatic feeders. I remember the time when we missed checking on our pigs for a few days. When we finally got down to the barn there was a terrible smell and it didn't take long to find out that one of our pigs had died some days back. We had to drag the pig out of the barn and bury it, but the body had decomposed so long that parts of the pig fell off as we dragged it out. Loving that "dead pig" is agape. "Agape" is loving something we see as worthless and putrid -- a smelly, disgusting mess that should be thrown away. God's love for us is agape love.

3. The Bible-- Important narratives – a "story" with many forms, illustrations and meanings. It is not a book of science... nor was it ever meant to be.

4. The Church-- Is Servant .... humble, taking orders. It represents Jesus on earth today. The Church should be retiring its buildings and assets... passing on these things to those who are the most needy.

5. Convicts-- MVPs Education and Rehabilitation We have been slowly moving in this direction mostly because of costs. We should be doing this for the sake of all people everywhere and for a more divine, creative world.

6. Our Idols-- Our idols should be destroyed like "the golden calf". Our most significant idol is Capitalism. Its focus is on self and greed –two of the most devastating crimes/sins against God and humanity. Capitalism is essentially a "survival of the fittest".

7. The World-- The world needs "leveling". All of creation (and especially human beings) need a leveling of "the playing field".

8. The Individual--l Putting the "self" or ego first is contrary to the Christian Faith. God's will comes first and instructs individuals to be equal to or serve others. Individuals are self-centered and sinful and so need "washing". The seed needs to die to itself in order to produce abundant fruit. In Baptism individuals are washed and forgiven... and so freed for service.

9. Creative Change-- Creative change is our "friend". This could represent the Holy Spirit in our world today. The history of the entire world is essentially a world living in, by and for change. God is creative change!?

10. Government/Politics-- This is where "the rubber hits the road" – essentially where words are meant to be put into action. Politics is living life in the midst of others. It is the way community functions –" living

life in the city." This is "practicing what we preach".

Notes -- Visits to jails/prisons... June 21, 2014 Started contemplating -- 3/22/2011 What I want to do on my visits...

1. I want to be a friendly, caring visitor from Eau Claire.

2. I want to convey a "nice to meet you" feeling -- you are a good and talented member of our society... having given and received significantly in your lifetime.

3. I want to say, "You are 'a very special person' with a very special and valuable story to tell -- one we all need to hear."

4. I need to tell you that I too am a "convict"... and facing that fact, with a lot of help, I can start on the path to becoming a better, happier more free person.

The above four are elaborated below........

1. Introduce myself as an interested, concerned, caring resident of Eau Claire... who would like to visit with a prisoner on a friendly basis. There are no expectations. It would be nice to share conversation regarding one or more of the following: feelings,

thoughts, information, ideas, perspectives, hopes, dreams, regrets, backgrounds, etc. -- anything that might be of interest to the prisoner. The visit might be very short or quite lengthy, depending upon how it goes.

2. I would like to extend good will toward the prisoner ("nice to meet you" flavor)... including my feeling that he or she is talented and important to society. Might there be anything the person would like to receive from one or more people... or would like to offer to one or more people... now or in the future? Everyone needs to receive good things from others, especially to mature as a human being. Sometimes we can be motivated to contribute something of ourselves (or of what we have) for the benefit of others. It's uplifting when an individual can feel a little better because someone has been good to them. We all benefit when people (even one by one) feel good about themselves, others and their surroundings.

3. It's important that I give the prisoner the clear message I think he or she is not only valuable to society, but is "a very special person". Being in a jail or prison, he or she is quite prominent and/or unique in "the path taken". The individual has

experienced something very important, which almost everyone desperately needs to contemplate -- something most people may not now know or recognize. Every person (especially prisoners) have an important, notable personal story going way, way back... about how he or she has arrived in this present time and place. It didn't happen overnight and there are a lot of important twists and turns everyone could and should be informed about. Change doesn't usually take place quickly... but it slowly and steadily moves us to act in certain ways eventually. We are creatures of habit... and tiny little inputs make each of us special and unique individuals. Each and every person can be moved over time (and the right circumstances) to do the most outrageous things. Yes, we make choices that affect our destiny. But it is equally true that every person can be moved over time (and the right circumstances) to do great and wonderful things. What is your story and how did you arrive in your present circumstances? That's a very special story to try to remember. We all need to hear it... for a lot of reasons. You are a VIP (a Very Important Person)-- yes, as a person... and in your unique experience! We can learn from your story!

4. If the opportunity presents itself, I would like to share a little of my hopes and dreams. It would be good and beneficial to all people that each and every one of us acknowledge that "we have a dark side" and with some help, it can be overpowered or pushed further and further away from affecting our lives. By acknowledging that fact, we all can increasingly minimize the chance of that dark side getting us into trouble or hindering our enjoyment of life. It would be great if every person could be in the process of rehabilitation and in touch with other people who can share of their experiences, reveal some of the pitfalls of daily living and maybe even offer some advice to those who want to be better people and get some ideas about how to do it. I consider change as a helpful and encouraging "friend". But change can only be helpful to a person who wants to go in a different direction. Really, because we all make mistakes big and small, we all are "convicts" in need of rehabilitation. Yes, I am a convict! Having thought about this for a few years, I've written an extensive book --"Convicts Cheer Change!" It lays out a path to recovery for all of us as "convicts"! We all need a lot of help and there are a lot of people with expertise who can help us. If only that could be understood and applied little by little in

our society today. Who would be better to tell us "what is detrimental or hurtful" than one who has experienced it? That's similar to a good parent teaching a small child "not to touch". Of course, learning can best be applied little by little, person by person, moment by moment... beginning even now. You can be "a change agent" for a better future in this very moment... with simply the "insignificant" decision to give it a try. Start by trying to remember "your story".

The Potential (Desired) Impact...

1. The prisoner is a happier person.

2. The jail or prison functions a bit more smoothly and efficiently.

3. The prisoner has better self esteem and is thinking about his or her past in a new way.

4. The community to which the prisoner returns has a little less to worry about... considering that he or she wants to do better.

5. The word gets out that something good can come out of "a guided time for self-analysis... a study of change... a re-evaluation of life goals... and learning how to be helpful in society". (The University/College of Change)

6. Families and friends of the prisoner have reason for pride in what he or she is accomplishing and realize hope for a better future.

7. There might be some encouragement and help provided by all levels of society (families, churches, businesses, political parties, schools, clubs, individuals, etc) as they begin to see benefits to society and come to understand how to help in this extensive process of education and change.

8. The prisoner coming out of prison/jail has an understanding of where he or she made detrimental moves in the past. He or she may desire to reveal those mistakes to others for their long term benefit. Everyone can gain for a better and happier life.

9. Concerned citizens living near a jail or prison might begin to understand how difficult it is to change the direction of one's life. They might offer to be friends, helpers, sponsors, benefactors, teammates, researchers, etc. for those on the mend -- inside or outside the jail or prison. It takes a community to change a life for the better, but everyone wins!

10. In the neighborhood, community, state, nation and even around the globe, people

might begin to be able to envision a world where no human being is disposable or beyond analysis, inspiration, help and concern. People have become "polluted" genetically, physically, mentally and spiritually... and so have suffered and deteriorated immeasurably. No person should ever be "locked in a closet"! We fellow human beings can learn much from people who have made big mistakes, even if and when they need to be confined for everyone's welfare.

My reasons to do "prison/jail visits"...

1. Set a goal -- something to do for others -- volunteer, contribute in some way, help.

2. Actually try to "work out" what I've researched and written about -- "Practice what you preach!" Do work I think I'm comfortable doing in the "nitty gritty" of people's lives.

3. Do some lifting up or giving (here and now) in an area of need -- hurting people, prisoners, prison system, etc. Try to experiment with a positive and special way of interacting with convicts.

4. Have interesting interaction with others -- "wrestle", discuss, think differently, change.

Be willing to talk about my books and what they bring to the table.

5. Carry out action without looking to receive financial gain... for the joy and blessing of it.

6. Attempt to be a bit more productive in the area of social interaction. Get more into social things and a bit more removed from material things.

7. Fill some of my days (in my declining years) with meaning and servant-hood as my spiritual leader would encourage. Get back into the ministry of love, forgiveness and hope.

8. In a small way, try to make the world a better place in which to live... hopefully for convicts, guards, families, community, etc.

9. Do something maybe only I can do... considering "my story" and the goodness I have received.

10. Stand up and face the real, hard, challenging, troubled world... with resolve and hope.

11. In making this effort, I would like to have my family, friends and community members see me acting more persistently on my convictions.

12. See if I can be a friend, in some sense, to individuals who may be looking for one.

13. Maybe find a way to get more outside of myself and my problems.

14. Face the fact that I can't reach all those who are incarcerated. Accept "a reality check" and a humbling experience... for the well being of my soul.

15. Be a "thank offering" to the world around me. Try to bring a measure of goodness, careful consideration, empathy and encouragement to those around me... as a thank you for all the blessings I have received throughout my life.

16. Hans Olson -- June 23, 2014

Miscellaneous items:

1. To the sheriff... Get his reaction to some ideas... At the Jail's "Open House" I talked to him briefly... appreciated his perspective on prisoners and rehabilitation. I've had two books published by Kindle Select, one being "Convicts Cheer Change!" -- it's 220 pages and about half on rehabilitation and our justice system. I self-published it about a dozen years ago. Essentially what I'm here for is to find out from you if it's OK to do

some "visiting" with the prisoners and start practicing some of my suggestions. (Show book; also show my Logo card; also the sheet certified by the State of Wisconsin and the Secretary of State) I've been a Lutheran minister, but I am not doing this to "save souls". I want to do this... to be able to simply help make this world a better place in which to live... starting in a jail cell. I telephoned the jail 7/29/13 in the morning; It was suggested that he would call me back... "...maybe next week".

2. It would be my ultimate goal that "down the road", convicts who are released would find ways to give back. They could offer excellent perspective to society (ways to fight crime) from the extensive study and training they have absorbed from prison -- The University of Change. They would be presented as VIPs (overflowing with ideas... each one with a unique perspective and story) who "know the ropes" and how to avoid temptations that move toward criminal behavior. Once prisoners, they could be applauded after "graduation" as changed, productive, admired role models. Who better to lead us in the "reconstruction" of our society?

3. I'm a bit ill at ease about my plan to visit

prisoners and to suggest some modest proposals. Words that come to mind about all this are... unorthodox, disturbing, silly, foolish, preposterous, un-American, risky, unworkable -- downright revolting! However, I'm a conservative, law abiding, comfortable, highly respected senior citizen that lives here in Eau Claire. I've received one ticket in my life and raised two sons I'm very proud of. I have a very important idea to suggest -- essentially for the rehabilitation of our society. We desperately need rehabilitation today; and if we have openness to look carefully, we have the natural resources to do the job.

I've studied change for many years and I've written two books -- one being "Fact or Fiction? Convicts Cheer Change!" This is a 200 page rather "unsettling book" about an urgently needed restructuring of our justice system in this country. I see today's jails/prisons as being the new highly respected elite colleges or universities of the future. Today's lawbreakers, criminals, convicts might be considered some of the most valuable people in any and every community. Impossible? All this starts with a simple but bold word of good news to people inside and outside of jails. Convicts could begin to see themselves as VIP change agents -- Very Important People in helping to create or recreate any healthy, happy, vibrant communities within our society. People outside prisons could be liberated from fear of the criminal who has served his or her time and furthermore, could look to that person as a resource for a better and more healthy community. All this perspective is not based on simply a wish or a dream or some other worldly experience, but on basic science -- as basic as "behavior modification" or evolutionary change. Nothing is more true than the fact that everything is changing and/or will change. The only thing that doesn't change is change itself.

Let's use a very basic, simple illustration -- let's "train" the maple tree growing in my front yard. This maple tree can be shaped or turned in any direction (over time) by constant pressure and positive stimulation. On its own, in a bad environment, it might grow in any direction; but put into a refreshing environment, with new restraints and new encouraging stimulants, that same tree, no matter what age, can be turned around to grow, function and produce its fruit in a whole new way. Like almost all of nature, human beings are very similar. We are "creatures of habit" for good or for bad. Our personalities are created from infinitely small, repeated impacts that one by one take us in a certain direction. Even our genetic code can be impacted for good or bad results. This is just basic science. Think about where the smoker, drug addict, gambler, sexual predator, etc. got started... and then little by little moved in the same detrimental direction, usually over an extended period of time. There's a very great chance that our diseases (cancer, heart attacks, etc.) also got started by very small influences or we might even say choices. To counter such things, training-- constant negative pressure plus continual positive encouragements (the carrot and the stick) -- done in a controlled environment can work what we might call "miracles"... again, usually over an extended period of time. Think about the convict, who could choose to have very strong, small, ongoing, scientific, positive and negative impacts in order to change the direction of his or her life. The right environment -- the University of Change -- could have a gigantic influence on a person. Contemplate the chance to start over, find small successes, receive a new vision of the future, be trained for new goals, be part of an exciting, successful team, gain increasing rewards -- these positive stimulants presented in the right amounts could change almost anything.

Where would I start? If the opportunity for a visit resulted in conversation, I would like to offer some good news... from my perspective... You are basically a good person... and you deserve better. You have insight that no one else in the world possesses, and that makes you special. You are what I would tell the world is a VIP (a Very Important Person) -- a person who we all need to see and hear... and should try to understand. It all starts with "your story" and how you have moved or traveled from where you were born to where you are now. I would guess that you wouldn't wish your present circumstances on your friends... or much of anyone. That's part of the specialness of your story and what you can teach all of us. What happened along the way (both good and bad)? What moved you or affected your life? What do you really like about that journey and what do you regret? Couldn't we all learn a bit from your experience? In a sense, that's what is so wonderful about good parents -- that they can teach their children both good and bad from their experience. That's crucial, if we truly want a good, healthy society... as well as to live in peace with one another and be happy with what we have. I think that's what we want for our children. Every day we all need to learn more about where the pitfalls are and about what's good for us. You have something special to share about all this and no one can ever take that away from you! Consider what it might be like to have a new productive, satisfying life with well deserved rewards, feeling good about yourself and living in happiness and contentment. All that can be trained and learned with some inspired help. But it starts with you and your story. That's personal and only you can think about it, understand it and let others know about it.

Why not take a glimpse at the potential benefits to such a modest proposal. Not surprisingly, they are "infinite" and could "turn the world upside down". If people could begin to understand (even from one small example) how real change can take place in a person, the multiplication of goodness and benefits would be "off the charts". Here's real liberation, freedom, re-creation, self-esteem, hope, forgiveness, renewal, transformation, higher education, friendship, respect, admiration, teamwork -- endless potential for good -- some might suggest a "Christ on the cross" revolution. It would start with looking at change as a friend not an enemy. It's a friend everyone needs for a healthy future. Yes, it would require people outside the prison to see life from another person's perspective -- in a way, a whole new way of looking at life. That wouldn't come quickly or easily, but consider the positives. People could learn from their mistakes (they could be liberated from being afraid of them and act more courageously) and gain a transformational humility. They could reap endless rewards learning from the experiences of others. And they could be liberated for exciting, healthy, transformed living. This could be learned and practiced -- all coming out of the University of Change.

If something like this could be started in the small jail cell, what in the future would be the cost of crime? What would incarceration mean? How could the environment within the jail change? How would society view the prison or the University of Change? Who might be the new "professors"? or teammates? or inspirations? What would be the loss from the present system of incarceration? The far-reaching questions are endless.

Really, this is "a modest proposal"! What's wrong with it? Any additional ideas or proposals?

T. Hans Olson --6/24/2014

Prison Visits... July, 2014

A bit more clearly... laying out the idea... "A focus on rehabilitation of convicts" From the book: "Convicts Cheer Change! c. 2001

Suggested reading...

1. p. 120-153 -- Chapters 11-14

"Criminals Becoming Crime Fighters" "Training Centers For A New Social Order" "Switching Sides For Success" "Community Rehabilitation"

2. p. 12-21 -- "Change Booklets" and

two letters to Ann Landers... regarding... "Criminals might be rehabilitated"... "Proposal for dealing with crime and criminals..."

3. p. 25-58 -- Chapters 2-4 -- Thinking about change...

"Change... From Grief To Joy" "Checking In... To Change" "Motivated For Change"

4. p. 196-202 "Ideas For A Program In A Prison"

Personal Information

Born in Mauston, WI 5/14/1942 Graduated from Mauston High School,

St. Olaf College, Luther Seminary

Served as a Lutheran minister 1967--1982: Dwight, North Dakota.
Birchwood, Wisconsin.
Spring Valley, Wisconsin.

Volunteer work -- Bread for the World

Married since 1967 and father to two sons

Author -- "Convicts Cheer Change!"
Self-published in 2001
Kindle Select -- 7/10/2013

Author -- "One Path To Peace In Palestine" Presented 2003-2004
Kindle Select -- 7/18/2013

Author -- "A Bible Story"
Self-published in May, 2006

See myself as ...

T HANS

Minister, Counselor, Writer, Reformer. Volunteer, Artist, Restorer, Modeler.
Photographer, Inventor, Collector.

Numerous hobbies and interests

I would like to make an effort to....

Help "hurting" people in prisons become
important assets to our communities. Make a move toward "upgrading" a jail or
prison to a University of Change.
T. Hans Olson 3037 Hartwood Drive Eau Claire, WI 54703

An Email To A Lutheran Minister

Email from T. Hans Olson 8/4/2014 (After reading his packet of articles -- "Politics & The Pulpit", etc. which he gave to me at a Bible Camp at the end of July...where he was a speaker.)

August 4, 2014
Presenting Pastor...

Where do I start? You presented me with quite a range of material. First, I want to thank you for taking time to listen to a self-proclaimed rebel. It's risky. Before leaving the parish ministry back in 1982, I wrote a 19 page statement voicing my concerns about the structured church in the United States. "Should I Leave The Parish Ministry" was sent to the District Presidents of The American Lutheran Church throughout the U.S. as well as to four seminary presidents. It challenged a lot of things. I received two letters. One seminary professor suggested that the manuscript contained issues that should be discussed among the clergy and other leaders. After presenting my paper at a conference pastor's meeting, the comment in response that shocked me the most came from a pastor who apparently spoke for many -- "What can I say? It's all true!" Yet generally the silence from the churches was deafening... and still is! I tell you this to simply let you know a little bit about my "history". Before I go on, I should mention that I think all the articles you gave me are instructive and to the point. I wouldn't quarrel with any of them. We have some of the same viewpoints.

It might be good for me to comment on what you presented Thursday night at Bible Camp. You have been able to continue in the parish ministry because you have known how to please at least a majority of church members. You told jokes and had people "in the palm of your hand". Your subject matter "Giving Thanks!" is probably the most loved and appreciated topic in the Christian Church. It's popular. I think it's right up there with "agape love"... as the New Testament explains the most important way to live a Christian life. I focused on my Dad's thankful life at his memorial service. We agree on the subject matter. But you didn't disturb or challenge much of anyone about what it really means to give meaningful thanks for new life... or make anyone really think about what it would take to stand on the side of the poor, etc., and everyone of us needed to be disturbed about our thanksgiving... probably especially at Bible Camp. Where do we give our offerings? To whom? Should there be any risks? Who did Jesus "take under his wing"? Who should give thanks focusing on "the least of these"? Did we leave the service giving much thought to what you said? I'll tell you that I was upset that evening concerning what you didn't say. Some religions ask their followers to give their lives in order to "get to heaven". We generously let people know that a person can pretty much get there with "Jesus loves me" and "thank you." Is that what should be called "cheap grace"? You avoided what is essential to following in Jesus' footsteps (a change in direction)... maybe because you don't believe that... or because you would no longer be popular... or you might not get called back to Bible Camp. We live our lives offering a polite "thank you". We go to church to "give thanks". We pray and sing to give thanks. We tell our children to give thanks. We give a little offering to give thanks (often to keep the church or bible camp in good shape). And we believe that thanksgiving will get us to heaven. But, for the most part, we don't give thanks in much of any meaningful way... any more than we carry out agape love or love our enemies, etc. What does the New Testament tell us, if we want to tell the truth? And because we don't tell the truth, the whole world loses out. "Christianity" in the capitalistic USA -- "God bless America"!? Yes, we may give some of our "crumbs" and we try to say all of the right words. What does that mean to outsiders? That's why the Christian faith doesn't carry much water in our world today. And that's why the Christian Church is in as much need of a Reformation today as it was in Luther's day. We have done almost everything with "The Word" except to move it into action -- to make it flesh again as we strive to be "little Christs". It could turn the world upside down... if the Christian Church became Christ's Spirit in the world today. What do we have instead? Not much -- some entertainment and emotional demonstrations! Actually, we've got the most radical and liberating message to tell and demonstrate, but we don't want anyone to really hear it or see it. Why? Because they might be disturbed in their daily living (as they go along with the crowd in our capitalistic, survival of the fittest system)-- they might be disturbed in their narrow Biblical views, in their self-righteousness, military mentality, materialism, aggressiveness, greed, addictions, gluttony, patriotism, anger, racism ... well, you know the list. Should I be sorry I'm so blunt... or maybe I'm confused... or a crazy man?

I need to move on, but stop reading right here if I'm being too negative for our time and place. The worst is yet to come! You are an insider. I can lay it out the way I see it because I am free from the normal restrictions in the average parish. That's good, in my way of thinking. My 200 page book (an ebook from Kindle Select), "Convicts Cheer Change!" (Fact or Fiction?) is about needing a re-formation of the Christian Church -- here and now -- and about the need for a total revolution in our "justice system" across this country (and really around the world). People in the future (if we have one) will look back at the way we do justice as "the dark ages". By the way, we are all convicts-- every one! What I've laid out is hard reading (emotionally), but two theologians who have read it have given no criticism. The book features change and suggests the way to get to a new place... for the church and for the prison. I won't go into details but one personal conviction will give you a significant insight into the presentation -- our church buildings in this "enlightened age" are the golden calves of the Old Testament. We spend our time around them, we enjoy them, we keep them looking pretty, we have our leaders keep them prominent in our priorities, we pay good money to build them, we are inspired by them, we keep them "spit polished", we give good pay to the "caretakers" as long as they say and do what they are told, we recruit worshippers, we can show others our comfortable pews... and above all, they help to distract us from what we were called out to accomplish through the power of Jesus Christ. Consider how the church and its leadership are unknowingly leading us down the path to hell on our planet. We shouldn't be so concerned about "getting to heaven" (like other religions) but about being good stewards of all that our creator and redeemer God has showered upon us. That is commendable thanks giving!

If that isn't enough, here's almost the ultimate "lunacy"! I have proposed a 10 point plan for peace in Palestine. One Path To Peace In Palestine is about a 70 page book published by Kindle Select last year. However, I proposed this and sent it to both sides back in 2004. I said at the end of my proposal that if there would ever be an enduring peace in Palestine that it would have to be a plan something like this. One needs to understand how "change" can work to realize how peace can truly be accomplished in that area of the world. This is a totally different way to get to an enduring peace -- really the only way. Set aside all the arguments you've ever heard from either side. Two basics are essential, and everyone (with the exception of the politicians maybe) will agree with them: 1. No enduring peace will ever take place unless the plan incorporates a long term process (too many people, too much history and too much anger, etc.) 2. Both sides in this conflict will receive exactly what they want... down the road a bit. (All the people of the Middle East will need to have hope that they will get exactly what they want, if they accept this 10 point plan.) Those two ideas are basic, and both Arabs and Israelis need to get the politicians (too much power and ego) out of the way in order to accomplish peace. I won't go into the total peace plan, but I know it will work because I understand people and I understand how change works best in God's world. Have you ever considered that essentially the whole Bible is about redemptive, life-giving change! Is that a bit of heresy or what?

I'd better quit... if you have gotten this far. I have tried to listen to the prophets over the years... and I have been troubled by even my own words. But I am not afraid or insecure in my convictions. I'm not even too concerned about people not wanting to listen. If Palestine wants to continue on its present path, the people on both sides will get what they deserve, sad to say. However, I am convinced that the Christian faith and the liberating love of Christ can turn even Palestine into a land of peace... and "flowing with milk and honey". Time will tell. We each have a chance to choose how we change for the advancement of Christ's love. Thanks for listening!

T. Hans Olson 3037 Hartwood Drive; Eau Claire, WI 54703

A Second Email To A Lutheran Minister

August 11
Presenting Pastor...

You would have been forgiven for not getting back to me. I knew it would take a very special person to even read all the way through my response. Having left the parish ministry a long time ago, I have no reason to hold back from expressing my convictions... although I do face the fact that predictably almost no rational human being wants to hear these things... myself included. I'm convicted by reading my own book! Right or wrong about most of what I loaded on you, being a rejected or lonely figure doesn't trouble me... living in our time and place. We have almost no voices willing to risk laying it on the line today -- politically or spiritually -- not unlike the church in Germany many years ago. Who wants to get hurt... as good as we've got it? But where does that leave us in this generation? Again, thanks for listening. There's no urgency for you to get back to me or even for you to make comments. However, I will now be a bit more optimistic about getting some feedback from within the structured church. Actually, truth be told, the Spirit (hopefully still within the church) is about our only hope. I hold out for a new re-formation, even though It's not even on the horizon. The person of Jesus Christ should not only be heard on the hillside, but seen, felt and experienced in the flesh. It wouldn't be easy to have him among us these days. Take care. Hans

An Email To A Cousin

From: Hans Olson
Sent: Thursday, November 06, 2014 2:01 PM Subject: God and politics

I just wrote to Mitch Albom asking whether he thinks the following "Letter To The Editor" should or should not be published in a U.S. newspaper. I also would like to hear what someone "close to me" thinks. You are that knowledgeable person. I have sent this to three newspapers -- one in Eau Claire, Madison and Milwaukee. It also went out to my wife, my sons, my brother, my sisters and one prominent Lutheran minister in Minneapolis. After the letter was "laid on my soul" election night, I struggled quite a while with whether or not I should send it out to anyone. I figured there could be some risks. Then it came to me that I had to act, regardless of the consequences. Something like this has been on my mind for a long time. I have received two comments so far -- "thanks for the message... I appreciate it." from the Lutheran minister, and "good!" from my wife, Marian. Could there be a "storm brewing" with regard to this, or is the letter merely a radical, irrelevant, stupid, heretical, unimportant comment for our time and place? My motive for writing this was to simply try to get people to think -- one tiny, little input... for maybe some future consideration. I'd be interested in your perspective -- no matter what you might have to say. Thanks for being who you are!

Evening of November 4, 2014
To interested citizens:

Our newly elected Republican Governor of Wisconsin -- Gov. Scott Walker -- walked up to the podium... and his first words were, "I want to thank God..." What a testimony! Isn't it wonderful for the state of Wisconsin and for our country as a whole that God has "switched sides"! He no longer stands on the side of the (lazy) poor and powerless, the (wasteful) hungry and homeless. He has finally "revealed Himself" on the side of powerful, "well to do" and wealthy people... as well as on the side of people who want, one -- more tax cuts for the wealthy, two -- big businesses to reap greater profits, and three -- more money for the military. Thank God that we Americans can have hope for a better future... and that the hard workers, executives and "paid for politicians" will have His power and aid to help in the struggle to get further ahead. Thank God!! God bless America! He (God) has finally gotten his priorities straightened out! What a relief it is! Hip, hip, hurray America! Point to the sky! You finally voted for a winner! Have a fun, profitable and happy Christmas!

T. Hans Olson

An Email To A Hunger Activist

On 3/11/15, Hans Olson wrote:

(Hunger Activist):
This is not easy for me to write, but you said, "I'd love to hear from you in any way that's easy for you." I deeply respect and applaud your great efforts over the years to speak and act for the poor and hungry, so instead of tossing your letter, I feel I should respond. My mother, Bessie Olson, was an early BFW member and urged all six of her children to become members. When I was in the parish ministry, I did almost everything I could to recruit members... with generally poor results. For the vast majority of church members today in this country, their political indoctrination trumps their weak spiritual knowledge, witness and commitment to Christ's friends. Consequently, the structured church around us is in serious trouble -- it may well be a downright hindrance to the Kingdom of God -- in a sense, leading us all to hell in a hand-basket. A feel good mentality! Words, words, words... buildings, buildings, buildings... golden calves, golden calves, golden calves... entertainment, entertainment, entertainment! Because of what the church has not done throughout the ages and especially

in these "terrible days", I blame the church for a good share of the evil in our world. The early Christian Church (followers of Christ) was given the greatest treasure mankind could ever receive, yet that Church has squandered and polluted agape so badly, it is almost unrecognizable in today's world. We know the various sicknesses and abominations that have filled the void here and abroad. The Church in Hitler's Germany was probably no worse than what the Church in the U.S. represents to the world at large. I almost literally tremble for the terrors that lie ahead. I left the parish ministry in 1982 after issuing some challenges. I am almost to the point that I don't want to be associated with those who call themselves Christian, point to the sky, shout "God bless America", push selfish, aggressive, violent interests, and even ridicule Jesus' friends. Having said all this, you can understand why I believe the Christian Church today is more deeply in need of a re-formation than at any time in history. Now, you have written your letter to receive support and finances for a great cause. We need both love and justice -- around the globe. Your efforts are not in vain, even though you have to listen to this. In a way, I'm sorry to present to you this perspective. But Jesus himself gave some indication of the un-attractiveness of The Kingdom of God. I would guess we probably agree that Jesus is The Way, The Truth and The Life... hard as His path is to travel. Take consolation that this response is probably one in a million. I am a rebel and hard to live with. My advice, if I would have any to give -- Be patient, sow seeds and struggle on toward the prize.

NOTES FROM "THE CATACOMBS"

For your records: My name is Thomas Hans Olson -- I sign my checks T. Hans Olson and I go by Hans. With the last name of Olson, I have always been happy to go by Hans. My mother's maiden name was Thomas. It's probably best that I'm not even addressed as Rev. I read every word of (your co-worker's) letter. I was "warmed" by his testimony and thankful for his commitment to BFW. I hope many other BFW members do the same. I am at the point in my life that I say to myself, "Every dollar I can save these days, I want to go to help those in real need." I have had a blessed and wonderful life. Believe it or not, I enjoy every minute of every day... yes, even writing this, since I think it's my responsibility to say it. Needs are evident in both love and justice. Sentimentally, BFW is more important to me than even my two beautiful, wonderful grandchildren.. in terms of passing on any future resources that I might have. However, I did not respond to (your co-worker) because I am not prepared to tell him or you at this moment what is in my financial future or exactly my priorities. I believe Jesus loves people into giving and sharing. Manipulating letters and messages come from every direction... and very rapidly in our day. I do have to live in my present environment and it has many challenges... given my perspective on a lot of things. Keep BFW on target and don't depend too much on today's church... or it may suck you in. Truthfully, (in this country) shouldn't every honest, informed, committed Christian be a BFW member?

I am guessing that you already know that we live in some tough times! How heartbreaking it must be to watch what's going on in Washington, given what wonderful possibilities there are at our disposal. It's even more appalling that what's happening there is simply a reflection of what's happening on main street. Still, isn't that the human condition for which Jesus came to offer Divine guidance and delivery? Praise God and the Holy Spirit of Jesus Christ! Every so often we can catch glimpses of Divine intervention... and I think that's what he cautions us about and urges us to look for... right? Thanks for your love, persistence and patience. A fellow servant, Hans

"A Position Paper"
-- July 28, 2015

Sideline: God works in mysterious ways... Today, I'm contemplating a new book... with this position paper being the final chapter. On Saturday, July 25, (down at Luther and Lindsey's) we were finishing our supper when Lindsey asked me a point blank question: "Do you ever go to church anymore?" I said, "No." Then she asked, "Is there a reason?" I said, "It's too depressing!" She answered, "Fair enough."

Today (as I'm about to start typing some recent thoughts... starting after talking with Luther for a while following the "Q and A" with Lindsey), I'm thinking of putting together some of my past statements and comments in an e-book form. The title would be, Notes from "The Catacombs". The title arises from some of the wording in this position paper. Given Luther's past help with my e-book "One Path To Peace In Palestine", it might be interesting to see if Luther would be willing to work up a cover for this e-book... down the road a bit. These are just some early thoughts, but saying this may encourage me a little to proceed with the idea -- a project that is troubling for me, to say the least. I thought I might/could be through with writing. It will take some time, thought and "wrestling with God" to see such a thing through.

Now, "The Position Paper"...
New Testament Christians are called by Jesus Christ to be...

1. "Little Christs". All so called Christians are called as disciples/followers to walk in Christ's footsteps, to act in his name, to do his work in the world, to try to understand God's will for their lives, to go against the ways of the world, to exhibit agape love, to not act in legalistic ways, to imitate Christ, to seek after doing his will in the world, to have a higher and more long term goal than simply an earthly one, to have a vision for an eternal destination, to be willing to listen and act on his pronouncements, guidance and suggestions, and finally, to live independently of the average, worldly point of view.

2. Peaceful people. Christ followers are not violent in any way. They show peacefulness in exhibiting Christ's love -- not revealing hate, superiority, blame or contempt. They refrain from conquest, always trying to seek ways to act in kindness and trying to heal wounds. It is their mission and goal not to hurt others, not to push away, not to punish, but instead try to build up and rehabilitate

when desired and appropriate. Protesting is always peaceful for Christ followers.

3. Forgiving people. In truly loving families, people forgive. Individuals in God's family (with Christ as the head) always try to be a blessing to others. They are not judgmental. They look to see the good in all people and refrain from putting people down. Where the world wants vengeance, Christ's rehabilitation process includes forgiveness, no matter what the crime. Loving means forgiving. Forgiving means forgetting and uplifting.

4. God's caretakers/Good stewards. Jesus Christ is the Creator God's only son. It is only appropriate and right that Jesus' followers seek to look after and build up the whole creation. They do this for the present and future joy of all things. They are willing to take less in order to cultivate the creation for growth, because they are indebted to the Son. Christians are not primarily concerned about themselves but look after the interests of even future generations... saving for others. Consequently, they do not act as though they own or control what they manage and they do not do anything that may be hurtful, greedy or wasteful. Christ's followers promote long-term fruitfulness

and look for ways to sustain life and the creation, minimizing selfish behavior every day. Everyone and everything in the creation benefits from good stewardship!

5. In renewal. God is not static -- He never has been and never will be! His Only Son is like God -- always working to be more in tune with His Father in Heaven. Jesus' followers have in their "genes" to be more like Him each day. That means daily change and renewal -- to continually be in the process of divine change. Being a Christ follower means to "never have arrived", to be continually open to newness, to be living in an active process of being redeemed, to learn flexibility, to live out a "daily baptism", to be continually offering the world a new image of divinity, to be open to divine insight and finally, to never be satisfied with what is static or what has been attained. The whole creation has always been in the process of change since the very beginning. The whole Bible is about change. What might we say about God? God should become more clear to us as we become more in tune with God's existence through Christ Jesus.

6. Servants. Jesus came to earth to reveal to us what it means to be a servant. Every one of

Christ's witnesses is also meant to act as a servant. This means... to be self-giving and self-sacrificing, to be like Jesus in serving others, to live a humble life, to minister to "the least of these", to be willing to give up excess (more than enough) for those in need, to do away with greed and overabundance, to give up pride and luxury for humility and generosity, to desire less of what the world wants to sell and to accept less power, authority, privilege and prestige.

7. Advocates for "new life"! Without Jesus, the world is in a death spiral. Yes, God is waiting patiently, but things have gotten worse. The world desperately needs "new life"... and fairly quickly! What does "new life" mean? It means existing, acting and proceeding in creativity... rather than in deterioration and destruction. It means encouraging the work of the Holy Spirit (Jesus' activities) to reveal a new way of living for everyone around the globe and for everything within our sight. It means carrying out the earth's activities differently than what "the world" recommends. "New Life" means struggling against the tide of competition, greed, violence, dominance and destruction, etc. Being advocates for new life means working to liberate all people living in slavery of any kind -- body, mind or spirit. Simply, Christ's

ministry means that every follower needs to be a nonconformist in the world.

8. Saved now and forever! Jesus doesn't promise us salvation to make us particularly comfortable in the here and now! Each of us is given a life to live and he expects us to struggle even as he did. But that life can be a truly blessed one living out our lives as his witnesses, followers and advocates. We are in charge of making decisions in our immediate lives. He is in charge of whatever the future might be for us... after we have lived our allotted time here on earth. Christ does not promise whatever we desire in paradise... so we must let it go! Forget the rewards! Christ's disciples had to. So how are we saved here and now? Be clear about this: We are saved by following "the way, the truth and the life". Jesus was, of course, "The Way, The Truth and The Life!" What could be said about "The Way" today? One must say that to seek The Way would be to seek a kind of global paradise where all people have their basic needs met -- body, mind and spirit. That certainly could be achieved by all nations living under the authority and leadership of Jesus, the Master. Christian fundamentals would be taught and learned at deepening levels, never to be fully attained in daily living. This unattainable

(in this present age) way of life is the way the creator meant (from the beginning) for his entire creation to thrive in peace and happiness. Although fully unattainable in our time and place, still there are concrete, practical ways for individuals, communities and nations to act out those Christ inspired characteristics essential for true happiness and fulfillment... today and forever. We can be saved to live in love (in Christ) now and for eternity. But each of is given the freedom to chose or not to chose to follow The Way.

And what does it mean to seek after The Truth? Basically, it requires that we are open to the truth wherever and whenever it appears -- coming from one like Jesus, from science, from faithful human beings, from the Bible, from nature or even from "space". Wherever more understandable truth is found, Christ's people want to absorb it and adapt to its implications. Why? Because Jesus is not only The Truth but also the way to The Truth... for everyone. We already know that the truth is continually growing and changing as time goes on. Jesus leads his people to true and lasting happiness through their faithfulness in continually being open to and coming into contact with as well as absorbing all there is to know.

And finally, Jesus is "The Life". In opening one's being to the Master of Life -- in acting out the fundamentals of new life and living -- a person can know and enjoy eternal life. This is not a "pie in the sky" reward for the world's view of living the good life, for being a good moral person, for being a good American citizen, for reading and studying the Bible, or even for faithfully following the church's teachings and going to church on Sunday. The Life Jesus offers all human beings is the life of the love he lived and died revealing --God's great gift to humanity.

Following the way, the truth and the life we learn to live our lives the way our creator intended us to live from the beginning. We learn to always seek out deeper truth about everything in God's universe, to have a sense of humility about one's condition, knowledge and perspective, to stay off any "high horse" we might have at our disposal, and in the end, to be about the mission of implementing "Good News" to all people.

The above eight fundamentals for Christian living are not meant to cover all aspects of a Christ-like life. They merely point to some critical aspects of Jesus' life and living. However, it must be stated clearly that these personality traits are all essential to what God wants for us and intends that we exhibit. They are all necessary for "New Life" in this world and they provide hope for ongoing gracious living in present and future generations. While the world is heading for deterioration, death and destruction, led by the law, competition, aggression, violence and a "survival of the fittest" lifestyle and mentality, the good news of the New Testament has the power and inspiration to bring about the radical change needed to save the world from chaos and destruction -- we might say, "hell in and hand-basket". True followers of Jesus Christ (not just

Palm Sunday cheerleaders and hopeful benefactors) have known about this divine solution to the world's suicidal race to extinction, but New Testament fundamentals showing the way to new life and hope for this planet have been hidden away, if not lost forever.

Let's look at the evidence of what our world is experiencing today. Naturally there are demonstrations of many religions, practice of religions not true to their own roots, reactionary religions and even individuals and groups who reject religions... possibly professing some kind of moral code for guiding life's decisions, hopes and dreams. Yet no religion or moral example has any recipe, road map or instruction manual for a redemption (re-creation, renewal, rehabilitation, salvation, etc.) of our planet. It's true that there are uplifting and redeeming exceptions to what can be seen in today's living. Many people around the world have pointed to the Christian Church as the world's only hope. What are the possibilities? The following evidence is admittedly a somewhat generalized perspective. Yet one must also remember that most churches are directed and run by simply a majority vote --that's our human democratic solution to an authoritarian approach of leadership. Essentially then, the masses run the show and, in fact, are basically what the world sees. The possible inspired minority are pushed away and are essentially invisible.

So what do we see in today's world? Where is the world headed and what are its chances for survival... if, in fact, the "Christian Church" is its only hope? Our evidence comes from today's so called Christians -- as in

"America is a Christian nation"... "God bless America!" These are the people claiming salvation through Jesus. So let's be honest. There will be no value in "sugar coating" what is happening. We are talking about life and death here -- for ourselves and for the planet!

1. Called to be "Little Christs"... Instead -- Acting like "Little Devils"... Too shocking? Untrue!? Again, let's at least try to be honest. Almost no one (in our day and age) wants to truly "follow Jesus". In fact, like the Devil, even individuals want to twist his words or change them into what they would like to hear. Radical action that got Jesus into trouble (like protesting government action, for example) is replaced by Bible Study or theological discussions -- words, words and more words. Christ-like love (caring for the bad, ignorant or disgusting) is replaced by punishment, neglect, incarceration and retribution. Being unattached to the world is replaced by being totally attached to the world -- wanting more than enough and plenty of insurance, greed, defense, military might, grabbing and wasting resources, taking and using what should be saved for future generations... the list goes on. Acting out convictions is replaced by minimizing or doing away with them. Trying to understand God's will is replaced by being happy God has given you the win or has taken your side.

Risking one's life giving love to foreigners is replaced by applauding those who are willing to kill defending our homeland's interests. Purely spiritual worship without materialism, structures, conveniences, comforts and security gives way to gaudy, plush, expensive worship centers that attract money for eternal reward, erasing debt, or for more pampering ministers and teachers. Defending the prostitute and criminal is replaced by condemning those who live differently. Living free of the law is replaced by promoting more laws to support personal interests. How can this add up to anything but acting like "Little Devils"?

2. Called to be peaceful people. Instead -- Turning out violent people. Our nation/culture promotes violence in sports, games, entertainment, hunting and defense. Even shopping sprees can turn violent. The biggest and most powerful military in the history of the world sells its destructive weapons around the world, uses and wastes unimaginable resources, kills countless innocents in foreign countries and even pushes for more power and influence in the world. This is all done in the name of a "Christian nation"! We do all we can for more domination in the world -- the goal is to be number one. We take pride in

having enough guns everywhere to protect ourselves and our assets. No sense taking a chance on giving up one's life in the land of the free and the home of the brave. Consider the type of violent, murderous, terrorizing, power hungry and blood-thirsty entertainment that is paraded before us and that we soak up as a "cultured people". We have superseded the jungle mentality in 20th century America! So it is in our nature to try to overpower evil (violence) with even more evil (violence). We get our training from base killer instincts that go back in history forever. It is no wonder that our opponents feel threatened.

3. Call to be forgiving. Instead -- Getting our revenge. It is commonplace in today's news to hear people talk about wanting "justice", and when it comes right down to it, they almost always want the greatest possible revenge or retribution. With a few exceptions, we want the wrongdoers punished. We want payment for bad behavior. I believe we think that then they will never do it again! Revenge brings on more revenge. Who wants to heal the wayward? Seeing the good in the criminal is usually seen as weakness. The world and every individual pays the price for this practice to go on and on. We really wanted revenge and punishment for 9-11.

We really wanted punishment for Saddam Hussein. We really want "justice" for killers of innocent people. The killing goes on and we seem to be amazed at it. Why does it go on and on? We will get our revenge, and of course, they will get their revenge. And the world struggles forward, hobbled, with less security, less happiness, less real contentment and less hope. We think all this works for us, and truly revenge does blend nicely with the world's fascination with evil. Revenge is just one part of our messed up "standard of living". No redemption here. No creativity here. No gift given here. No new insight here. No hope here. No forgiving here. We get our revenge.

4. Called to be God's caretakers. Instead -- Mismanaged ownership. Today we earthly inhabitants, acting as owners of the world and all its resources, have grossly mismanaged the whole planet. We have raped and pillaged the earth at every opportunity... for our own gratification and amusement. National ambitions have dominated history and every generation of every country has taken as much as it could to satisfy its professed needs. If these so-called owners of the world could find a new planet every few hundred years, we might not be in such a predicament. But

we have one world for one eternity and we have acted like spoiled two year olds. We fight among ourselves, we want what the other has, we misuse, break or cast aside our toys only to want new ones at every chance we have. Our environment suffers loss of practically everything good and healthy -- water, land, clean air, wasted resources, serious decline and extinction of many of the world's inhabitants, drastic, deteriorating impact on weather patterns, the creation of weapons that could destroy the earth as we know it, nations and peoples being ignored, mistreated, killed or starved to death, and to top it all off, we the first world powerful people attempt to increase our advantage, power and wealth. Others watch and wait. Some, of course, do not wish to wait, so they take every opportunity they have to storm a comeback and get their retribution. Yes, there seems to be chaos all around with no real peacemaker or guiding hand to pull things together or help the owners grow up. What a mess! Mismanaged ownership seems to be an understatement. Instead of building up the creation we have grossly torn it down... even for ourselves... today. Our greed and wastefulness is beyond anything the world has ever seen. Our near-sighted, selfish behavior has naturally caused an uproar... along with an even more dangerous and destructive contemplation --that of the rest of the family wanting to be just like us. Billionaires and lottery winners are the center of attention in our closed minded world of more, more, more. What do you suppose the real owner thinks? What action would you take?

5. Called to be in renewal. Instead -- Egotistical destruction. I can remember hearing church members affirm that they didn't want to say different words in The Lord's Prayer. We go from that triteness to the comfortable pew conviction that we are saved. "It's done!"... today's popular preacher proclaims! Yes, we have such a generous, graceful, understanding God. Really? Are we such static, blind, closed minded, "blockheads"? Let's get real! Who wants to be shaped to be a more useful, forgiving, humble, peaceful, joyful follower today? There may not be a more common desire in the US than to be more in charge, powerful, wealthy, educated and looked up to. Haven't we all egotistically graduated from taking lessons on how to be servants? Slaves and women used to learn those roles -- gone!... forever!? We are frozen in our worldly ways... and our egotistical wisdom is as dead as a doornail. All our worldly wisdom has done is brought us to the edge of death and destruction. How

close are we... to being in the process of offering a new image of divinity, to being dissatisfied with what "the others" want, to being open to New Testament insights, to living out a daily cleansing, to continually want to be molded more perfectly and to seeking out the process of being a redeemed child of God? That would be the meaning of being in renewal. Egotistical destruction is the opposite and very evident in our culture.

6. Called to be a servant. Instead -- Wanting to be # 1 There's a little passage in the New Testament about the Son of God taking on the role of a servant. THE #1 is acting out or performing the very lowest and most humble of duties. Now that's something to protest, and of course, the disciples did. We contend such actions just can't be the right way to go about living life today. That's not the way the world works! How true! We all want to be number one... at least in our heart's desire. And that's what "kills us"... and our relationships... and our governments... and everything in the world! Wanting to be number one is... doing whatever it takes to overpower, taking joy from others, using what others need, and soaking up privilege and prestige. Truly, it's pride and prejudice, it's greed and luxury, it's overabundance and it's self-glorification. "Wanting to be

number one" is the very opposite of actually being a servant.

7. Called to be advocates for "new life". Instead -- Increasing death. Death is in the news -- all over the world, not just in the United States of America. The human race has found many ways to bring about a lot of death and destruction. Even the religions of the world have caused their fair share. But the world sees no other option than increasing death. In fact, the world might imagine that increasing death could well be our salvation! How messed up is that? The increasing deterioration and death of plant life, animal life, say nothing of human life has caused us some concern... and maybe we might feel some need to tweak our nasty behavior. But increasing death seems to be as certain for our planet as the setting sun. No one has it figured out. It's just one sad and bad event after another increasing death. No creativity here! Just the same frantic competition, greed, violence, military buildup, materialistic domination and lame excuses for it all. Surely science will find an answer... to death!... increasing death? The human race has united in lock-step, conforming in every worldly way to the jungle mentality (the jungle lifestyle) that has us all going to extinction at an ever

faster pace. Yes, there's increasing death. How long do we have for living on our planet?

8. Called to live out The Way, The Truth and The Life.

Instead -- Having our way, our ignorance and our destruction. It's true that we have things going pretty much our way. After all, there isn't much desire for anyone to ask for direction. In our life decisions we simply want to adjust our sights and maybe try to make some corrections, if not just do the same as last time, maybe with only a little more effort. We all are a real "bull headed bunch", and our egos get in the way of us being told anything. So much for religious insights and directives. After all, what has God done for me lately? The way we live today is "our way" and given the fact that all people are very similar, the whole world's population is doing just... what feels good, what we have done in the past and what our minds tell us is logical. Of course, that's what we have all learned since we were kids and what the whole world has told us. It's no wonder that our corporate life activities have put us in "a real pickle." Live life for yourself, do your own thing, fight for your rights, get everything you can and help yourself. That's honestly the life we have chosen and work out moment by moment, even if it is given by default.

Could all of the above be considered ignorance? The history of the world has certainly made us aware that selfish and egotistical activities do not produce a happy, fruitful and fulfilled planet. But we have not even dreamed of a different course of action. Now, that is true ignorance! In recent decades, truth in science has tried to clue us in that we are headed for disaster. But on we go, knowing of course that we are saved! Could that be considered ignorance? Generations have shown that the way to a bad ending is going down the path of the jungle mentality or the survival of the fittest. There's maybe an even more seductive phrase -- going down the path of "consumer capitalism" -- getting everyone in the world moving more rapidly into greed and selfishness. This truly is ignorance of the first order.

What is the life we now live? Clearly, it is destructive. Do we feel secure? Do we have enough material things to live in happiness and fulfillment? Is this world a good place for our children and grandchildren to grow up? Do we have good health -- body, mind and spirit? Do we have meaningful work? Do we have stress? Do we have enemies? Do we have negative feelings toward any individuals, peoples or countries? Are environmental conditions getting better? Are world problems being worked out peacefully and productively? Are we happy with our political system? Need I go on? The life we now live is deteriorating rapidly toward death and destruction. We do not know The Way, The Truth or The Life. Have we even heard of Him?

This is a "Position Paper", so I must make my position clear. The so-called "Christian Church" has talked about Jesus for a couple of thousand years, so in a sense, we have heard of Jesus. We are told, He's the one who came to give us salvation by dying on the cross, so that all we need to do is believe in Him and we will be saved. It's simple and easy... if you come to the meetings, follow the church's rules and pay up. You do that to take care of one's churches (idols) and the custodians. In fact, for some time in history, a person could almost buy his or her way into heaven. Yes, we have heard of this man, Jesus, but as a man who called people to almost literally follow in his footsteps (act out his way of life), no, that man was buried away in The Catacombs -- seemingly, never to be found again. The words about him came off the cross (as a victory for us), but the actions (what got him crucified) they were lost or put to rest, possibly forever!

It's not so strange that this happened. Jesus' help, healing and kindnesses were quite popular, if you were on the receiving side. He had quite a following. But even the disciples had a tough time getting into the action... of protesting, going after the religious elite, turning the tables on the money-makers, getting on the good side of hardened and convicted criminals, cozying up to the prostitutes and sinners, rejecting the government's practices and showing people His connections to His Father. No, Jesus was not popular for his actions, as wise as those actions turned out to be in his day. It's no wonder that kind of unusual activity was "shoved underground".

But let's go back to those 8 fundamentals of truly Christian activity... as the New Testament lays it out... in its early documentation. Really, there aren't many church people that would argue those fundamentals are a bad recipe for a good life, and happy, healthy living for everyone on our planet. What's wrong with walking with a real reformer and getting a little separation from the wildness of the world, as well as having some peaceful living, forgiving people, taking better care of our planet, doing some changing for the better, getting some service work done, pointing out some new, refreshing ideas about living out a fulfilling life, and then finally, getting right down to finding out the truth... and living out a refreshing, creative and fulfilling kind of life? What's wrong with all that? Of course, our worldly condition would be that everyone else would also need to go along with these new ideas.

Jesus wanted a far better world for everyone to live in. He was after real freedom, not a lot of restrictions. He wanted people to be happy and he apparently handed out some good wine. He wanted people to accept one another and not to get into the game of judging them. He was all for peace and for every person having enough. That's real security! And even if we are bullheaded today, deep down, don't we really want to know the truth about things? There was really a lot of good stuff in what Jesus proclaimed as "The Way, The Truth and The Life"! Being a servant could be tough to take, but if others might be inspired to take on the role, who would lose? Actually, the kind of life Jesus was advocating was not bad, in any sense of the word. It was just pretty different than what people were used to and they couldn't wrap their minds around the idea that it could work. By instinct, we are creatures of habit and deeply ingrained habits are hard to break. So the world carries on, and pretty soon, even those who sort of remembered the way Jesus lived really had forgotten the revolutionary saving life and living Jesus demonstrated. It was so much easier to accept the package of a saving cross, forgiveness for all our inadequacies and a rewarding life in paradise. After all, isn't that really pretty close to what all the major religions promise the faithful? How different is our faith?

Moving on, the lot harder task is to examine the way we have lived "the Christian life". We have essentially corrupted those 8 New Testament fundamentals in our daily living and lifestyle. It's not really necessary to go over the way we have lived INSTEAD of carrying out the call of Jesus. We are all too aware of the messed up world we live in. And there isn't one of the established fundamentals we have even attempted to emulate. Why not? After all, most of us somewhat connected to the Christian tradition (those of us who have heard the words about the man Jesus) would probably assert with some credibility that Christ's example is the one actually lived out presentation that would work to bring about new life for the whole world. We so called Christians have been shown the example (the almighty, creator God has wonderfully wrapped real love into a human package and shown it to us), but in having seen this example in real life we have tossed the Chosen One (the Master) aside... to focus on our own amusement. Now most of the world has at least some excuse for not knowing The Way to The Life. The excuse would be ignorance, and it would seem to be a pretty valid one. But what about those of us in the traditional church (the corrupted, paradise promising one) who have at least heard the words about this Jesus Christ -- this Son of God who desires all people to, in a very real sense, return to paradise? What excuse or excuses do we have, other than that we are just spoiled "2 year olds" (spoiled brats) that just like "the world" better? Now this is not a pretty picture for those of us who have liked to think of ourselves as God's people and lord it over other poor souls as a saved Christian nation? It's true that we don't need to listen to all this, but of course, then we are left with no possibilities other than eventual destruction and death. Do we really think that our self-centeredness and greed will save the day... with science and our brains leading the way? Basically, even the devil knows when he is at the end of his rope! If we have come this far in listening and acknowledging our rebellion and guilt, then we have at least a chance.

Today (I'm starting to put down these words on August 1, 2015), there are at least some people that have a feeling we human beings are headed in the wrong direction. The pope himself seems to think the church should be doing something different than making pronouncements. Could he be getting into the action a little? We'll see. In any case, with all the bad stuff that's going on in the world, it's possible that the our human race could come to our senses and look for some kind of a savior. That doesn't seem to be in the cards for happening any time soon, but once in a while things get desperate enough for us to almost literally cry out for help. But where should we go for help?

The structured church should be way past

embarrassed about its past. Look honestly at the way we've handled the calling of Christ. I believe it can be established that this church we have so adored for a couple thousand years is in fact responsible for the terrible condition of the world today. The devil is having a hay day! If an institution like the church has "the keys of the kingdom" at its disposal (in other words, it has not only the answer for the world's problems but also has the solution to finding a kind of paradise again) -- if the church really has "what the world needs now is love sweet love" and then it goes and buries those "keys" and forgets about them, who or what should be blamed?

There has been one gigantic void in the world... forever. The one gift that could have made the difference in erasing this void was killed and buried. His way of life -- shown to us by God himself and revealed in its fundamentals as a radically different way to live -- was buried with Him. Jesus was killed because he would not give the people around him what they wanted. After his death on the cross, most of these same people figured that now they could receive from His Spirit what they had always wanted -- eternal security. He had died so that they could go to heaven! Certainly that was what it was all about. All they needed to do was confess that "Jesus is Lord" and they would be on his team as well as receive their reward. How convenient was that? The church leaders conveniently invited everyone to listen to his interesting stories, get on the bandwagon of pointing to His saving grace, be comforted in times of struggle and difficulty and in the end get saved for eternal happiness! Nice! Of course, the church found it useful to add on a few conditions, but all of that just made a lot of worldly sense. Meanwhile, his words were increasingly used for evangelizing, sermonizing, singing, worshipping and theologizing, while his life and calls to action were explained away, tossed aside, sometimes ascribed to saints and essentially relegated to historical footnotes. So now what could a restless, material, pagan world do with this spiritual void established by the so-called Christian Church? The world responded naturally, finding good competition and value in other religions that would vie with the church for saving souls. Now, everyone could get rewarded if they just followed their leader's teachings. How in the world could the world get a better hearing and propagate its false doctrines than through competing religions... issued to the highest bidders? Meanwhile, Christ's lifestyle and actions were deemed unworkable and useless in the real world. And so the void was filled with a lot of seductive, popular, legalistic, grandiose, prophetic, empty religions. That resulted in much more competition for the hearts and minds of people -- people without the basics for healthy living and people who had almost no hope for anything fulfilling or good in their lives. What an opening for those zealots who could call out these multitudes to sacrifice their "worthless, unhappy lives", not only to get great returns in heaven but also to be shown a way to get back at the "haves" on the planet -- the obviously corrupt crowd displaying evil around the world. Even today this religious fanaticism turns out to be an easy sell to a good share of the world's population.

Obviously there is a price now to be paid for our

negligence of revealing and living in touch with The Way, The Truth and The Life. More than two thousand years of corrupting the Good News has taken its toll. These days, the supposedly Christian and non-Christian world haven't a clue as to how to correct the world's decline toward disaster. The pace just quickens... and almost daily we witness more and more chaotic and terrible signals of evil, detrimental, deadly activities. Seemingly almost any "bad move" by any small group or even a powerful leader could tilt the scales toward an irreversible conclusion to life as we know it. How sad, when for generation after generation, the proper way to live creatively and joyfully on this planet was available and accessible to at least a small segment of those who knew about Jesus' life and activities.

It would be sad to conclude this "Position Paper" with merely a statement of the church's failure and evil deeds. That case having been made, there is still The Truth that the church has fairly reliable testimony in the New Testament. For the most part, history is quite clear as to who Jesus truly was as a man, who he acknowledged he represented as he lived out his short life, who he wanted to be his followers and who he called to be blessed, fulfilled and happy and as the creator God's people on this planet. No one was to be left behind. Everyone was to be freed and uplifted. His answer to essentially all the world's problems was in eternally living out the way of love -- God's love, agape love, self-giving love, boundless love, caring love, redeeming love -- the love He willingly and actively showed in his daily life. For God so loved the world.

So what could be done today, to reverse this disastrous, deadly slide toward chaos and destruction? Maybe, we should say, "What can be done...?" Prepare yourself for a reversal! We are talking about radical actions here and not about practical, reasonable adjustments.

1. As a signal to the world of a change of heart, inspired by the life of Jesus Christ, any church wanting to carry Christ's name, willingly and joyfully deeds all its buildings and resources to "the least of these" -- and more specifically to those most desperately in need of food and shelter around the world. NEWNESS

2. Christ followers commit themselves to rehabilitating all convicts with insight, love and compassion... in all jails and prisons nearby. DEDICATION

3. The community of the faithful meet together in small groups with the intent to support one another, give thanks to God for his goodness to the world, and finally to act as resources for outreach -- offering specific gifts with "Good News" to all people. WORSHIP

4. Individuals who honestly want to be "little Christs" get more fully into the process of learning how to exhibit Christ-like love to

all people and how to live creatively with all living things on our planet. LIFESTYLE

5. New Testament people (people who truly want to advance Christ's Kingdom on earth) commit to clarifying Christ's mission of revealing God's "Good News" to all the world's inhabitants... as well as invite them all to join in such efforts. EDUCATION/MISSION

6. That all servants of Christ join in celebrating and rejoicing in God's activity on earth. The atmosphere is filled with thankfulness, satisfaction, joy and pleasure in creative fulfillment -- body, mind and spirit. (i.e. eating, drinking, singing, affection, sexual enjoyment, sensual delights, etc.) CELEBRATION

Conclusion

We live in a troubled and anxious world. In our time and place, many of us are concerned if not pessimistic about the future quality of life for human beings... as well as for the condition/health of our planet (continuing to be an attractive environment for all living things). Most people truly care about their children and grandchildren and want good, satisfying, pleasant and happy lives for them. Since we have not been motivated to think about the kind of world that is sustainable and that promotes a healthy, pleasant, productive, peaceful environment for all people, we simply go on with our lives as we have in the past and trust that somehow, someway, everything will work out in the future. Clearly, that ignores the facts of life in today's world and at best is wishful thinking. We are getting very close to the brink of disaster, from which there may well be no return. The blame for this situation rests totally on humanity, and consequently, on each and every human being alive today. We act like owners of the earth and certainly are the dominating force on our planet. If we could be interested enough to get to the root of our rebelliousness (or why we live as spoiled "two year olds"), we would probably have to look at selfishness, arrogance and greed. So, listen to this... if you have a brain for contemplation: We can't continue to live our lives as tiny terrorists in our own little playhouse. There's no question that today's national interests have almost no regard for "the foreigner" --lying at the side of the road. We use our "self-defense" toys to keep the peace as long as the rules of the fun and games are in our favor. In our exclusive, first world eating, drinking and partying, we almost literally are getting away with gross negligence and the murder of countless people around the globe. We accept the fact of billionaires living proudly and freely in a world that tolerates and justifies abject poverty. In fact, many would like to be billionaires. In our middle class non-attentive, polluting, wasteful habits, we are in the process of destroying one another and the world as we know it. Yes, it's probably as simple as all that. When will we fall flat on our faces in a drunken stupor? When will we face up to the facts of our existence?

If there will be a long term future for the human race on this planet, there is no doubt that our species needs to be inspired (by the Holy Spirit?) to look at the best way of life attainable for human beings. We surely will need inspiration if we are to establish a creative balance purposely maintaining all life on earth. Really, there are not a lot of credible choices that arise out of the history of humanity. Where are guidelines to be found that take into account our human limitations, a world that needs to be protected and treasured, a perspective that has high regard for every human being, a way of living for creative and caring cooperation and rehabilitation, as well as divine values that exceed this world's basic survival instincts? It's worth repeating. There are not a lot of credible choices.

Although the church of the last two thousand years has failed miserably in liberating mankind from deterioration and destruction, still that same church's prime mover can be called upon to lead all nations toward the promised land. Yes, Jesus Christ was put to death on a cross, signaling mankind's unhappiness and rejection of his humble, self-giving, creative, spiritual and divine perspective. Humanity wanted its own way... and consequently put him down in order to do it our way. Then we promised ourselves infinite rewards playing church. What has it done for us... other than make us idol worshipers, aggressive, defensive, arrogant, selfish, foolish, judgmental and nearsighted? But, truth be told, his Holy Spirit can be brought forth from "The Catacombs" to guide today's world in acting out "The Way, The Truth and The Life". This divine Christ can lead the nations in setting forth the whole world's rehabilitation and renewal for a much brighter future. So be it!

T. Hans Olson --September 6, 2015

www.ingramcontent.com/pod-product-compliance
Lightning Source LLC
Chambersburg PA
CBHW020511030426
42337CB00011B/326